PIANO • VOCAL • GUITAR

R&B BALLADS

D0707504

ISBN 0-7935-7182-0

HAL•LEONARD® CORPORATION
7777 W. BLUEMOUND RD. P.O. BOX 13819 MILWAUKEE, WI 53213

CIVIC CENTER

Visit Hal Leonard Online at
www.halleonard.com

CONTENTS

4   **Ain't No Mountain High Enough** — *Marvin Gaye & Tammi Terrell, 1967 / Diana Ross, 1970*

10   **Ain't Nothing Like the Real Thing** — *Marvin Gaye & Tammi Terrell, 1968 / Aretha Franklin, 1968*

14   **Ben** — *Michael Jackson, 1972*

18   **Do You Know Where You're Going To?** — *Diana Ross, 1976*

24   **Easy** — *The Commodores, 1977*

30   **Got to Be There** — *Michael Jackson, 1972*

33   **How Sweet It Is** — *Marvin Gaye, 1965 / James Taylor, 1975*

36   **I Hear a Symphony** — *The Supremes, 1966*

40   **I Heard It Through the Grapevine** — *Gladys Knight & The Pips, 1977 / Marvin Gaye, 1968*

44   **I Second That Emotion** — *Smokey Robinson & The Miracles, 1968*

48   **I'll Be There** — *The Jackson 5, 1970*

53   **If I Were Your Woman** — *Gladys Knight & The Pips, 1971*

58   **Just My Imagination** — *The Temptations, 1971*

63   **Let's Get It On** — *Marvin Gaye, 1973*

70   **Maybe Tomorrow** — *The Jackson 5, 1971*

74   **Mercy, Mercy Me** — *Marvin Gaye, 1971*

77   **My Girl** — *The Temptations, 1965*

82   **Never Can Say Goodbye** — *The Jackson 5, 1971*

90   **Reach Out and Touch** — *Diana Ross, 1970*

94   **Smiling Faces Sometimes** — *The Undisputed Truth, 1971*

85   **Someday We'll Be Together** — *Diana Ross & The Supremes, 1969*

98   **Still** — *The Commodores, 1979*

102   **Three Times a Lady** — *The Commodores, 1978*

108   **Time Will Reveal** — *DeBarge, 1983*

111   **Touch Me in the Morning** — *Diana Ross, 1973*

116   **The Tracks of My Tears** — *The Miracles, 1965*

120   **What's Going On** — *Marvin Gaye, 1971*

126   **Where Did Our Love Go** — *The Supremes, 1964*

131   **You're All I Need to Get By** — *Marvin Gaye & Tammi Terrell, 1968 / Aretha Franklin, 1971*

138   **You've Made Me So Very Happy** — *Brenda Holloway, 1967*

134   **You've Really Got a Hold on Me** — *The Miracles, 1963*

AIN'T NO MOUNTAIN HIGH ENOUGH

Words and Music by NICKOLAS ASHFORD
and VALERIE SIMPSON

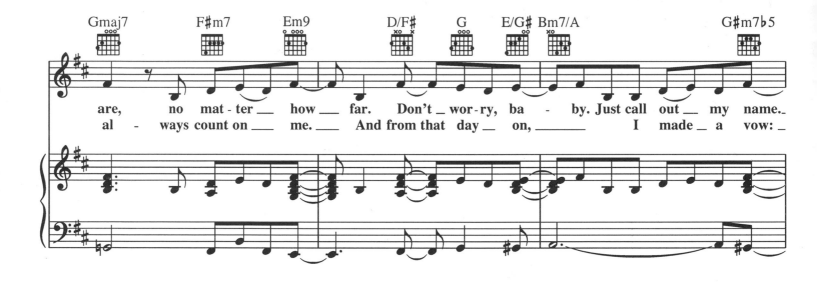

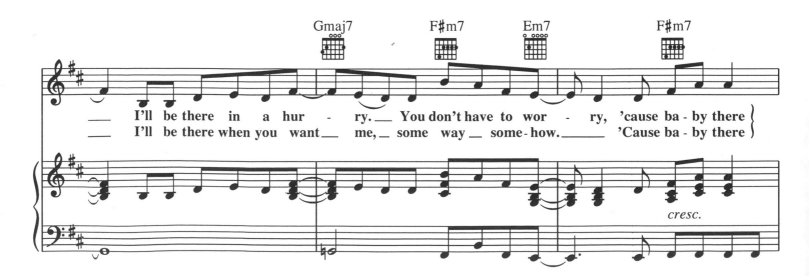

Eb maj

I'll be there on the dou - ble __ just as fast as I can. __ Don't you know that there

ain't no moun - tain high __ e - nough, __ ain't no val - ley low __

__ e - nough, __ ain't no riv - er wide __ e - nough __ to

keep me from get-ting to you, __ babe.   Ain't no moun-tain high __ e-nough,

no chord

AIN'T NOTHING LIKE
THE REAL THING

Words and Music by NICKOLAS ASHFORD
and VALERIE SIMPSON

in my ear. __ Don't you know, __ ain't noth-ing like the real thing, ba - by.
be-ing there. __ So glad we got the real thing, ba - by.

To Coda $\oplus$

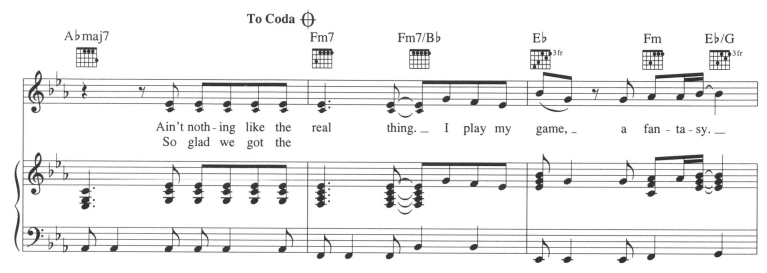

Ain't noth-ing like the real thing. __ I play my game, __ a fan-ta-sy. __
So glad we got the

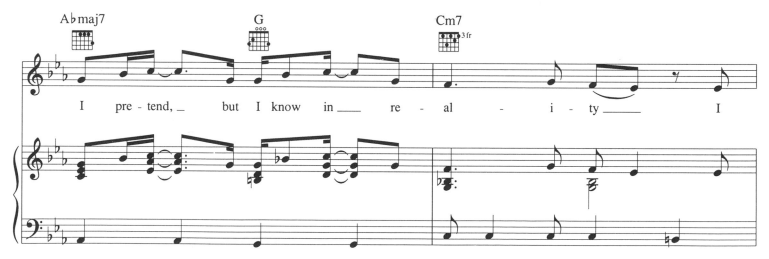

I pre - tend, __ but I know in __ re - al - i - ty __ I

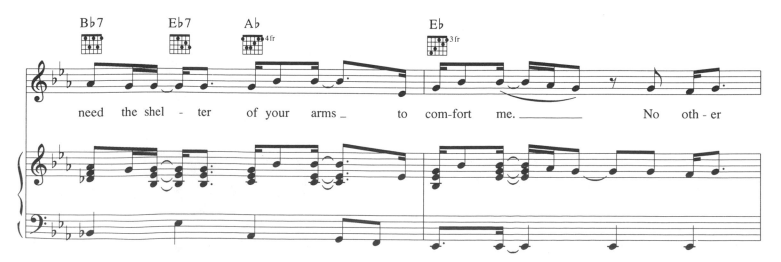

need the shel - ter of your arms __ to com-fort me. __ No oth - er

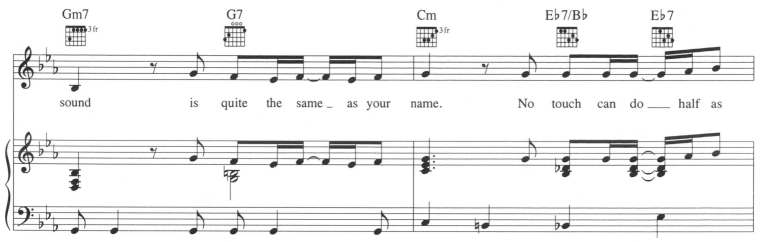

sound _____ is quite the same _ as your name. No touch can do _ half as

much _____ to make _ me feel bet - ter. _____ So, let's _ stay to -

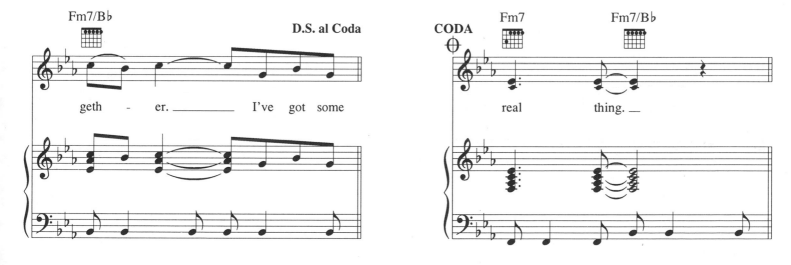

geth - er. _____ I've got some   real   thing. _

D.S. al Coda

CODA

Repeat and Fade

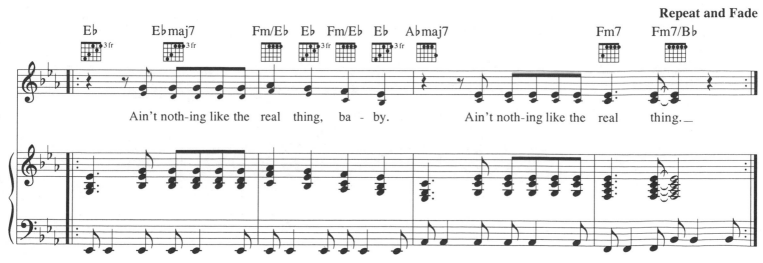

Ain't noth-ing like the real thing, ba - by.   Ain't noth-ing like the real   thing. _

BEN

Lyrics by DON BLACK
Music by WALTER SCHARF

Ben, the two of us need look no more. We both found what we were look-ing for. With a friend to call my own, I'll nev-er be a-

know. You've got a place to   go. _____   I

used to say   I and me.   Now it's us,

now it's we. _____   I used to say   I and me.

Now it's us,   now it's we.   Ben,   most peo-ple would turn

DO YOU KNOW WHERE YOU'RE GOING TO?

Theme from MAHOGANY

Words by GERRY GOFFIN
Music by MIKE MASSER

22

EASY

Words and Music by
LIONEL RICHIE

Know it sound fun-ny, but I just can't stand the pain; __

girl, I'm leav - ing you __ to-mor-row. _____

Seems to me, _ girl, you know I've done all ___ I can.

I wan-na be free, ___ just ___

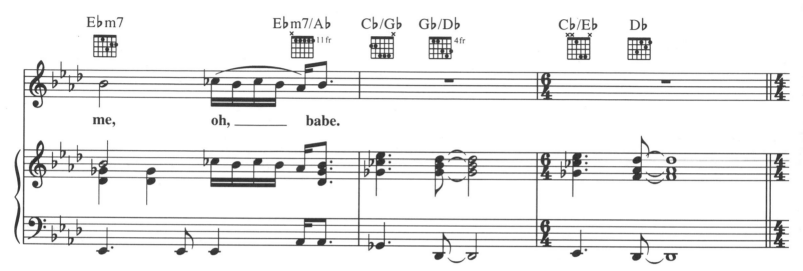

me, oh, ___ babe.

Instrumental solo

Solo ends **That's why I'm eas -**

GOT TO BE THERE

Words and Music by
ELLIOT WILLENSKY

HOW SWEET IT IS
(To Be Loved by You)

Words and Music by EDDIE HOLLAND,
LAMONT DOZIER and BRIAN HOLLAND

You were bet-ter to me than I was to my-self, ___ for

Coda

me there's_you and there ain't no-bo-dy else._I want to stop and thank you

ba-by;__ I want to stop and thank you ba-by, yes I do,

repeat and fade

How sweet it is ____ to be loved by you.

I HEAR A SYMPHONY

Words and Music by EDDIE HOLLAND,
LAMONT DOZIER and BRIAN HOLLAND

You've giv-en me a true love, and ev-'ry day I thank _ you, love,

for a feel-ing that's _ so new, _ so in-vit-ing, so ex-cit-ing.

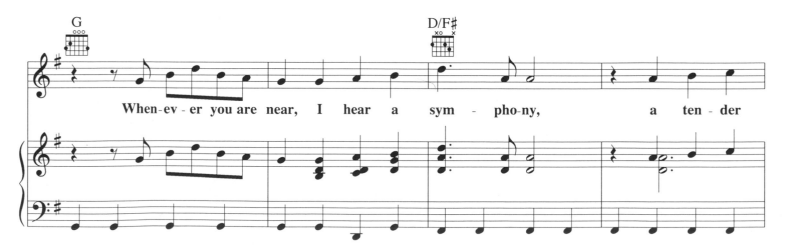

When-ev-er you are near, I hear a sym-pho-ny, a ten-der

mel - o - dy ____ pull - ing me clos - er, clos - er to your arms. ___

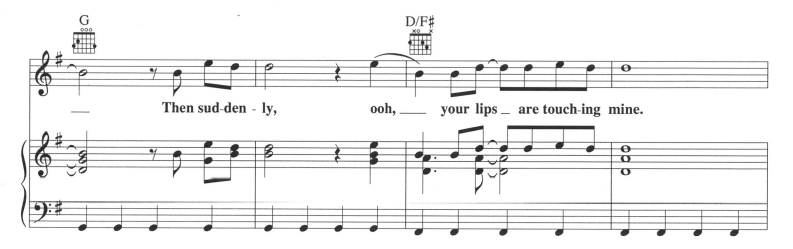

___ Then sud-den - ly, ooh, ____ your lips __ are touch-ing mine.

A feel - ing so __ di - vine __ 'til I leave __ the past __ be - hind. ____

I'm lost __ in a world _____ made _ for you and me. Ooh,

love me. _ When-ev-er you are near, _ I hear a

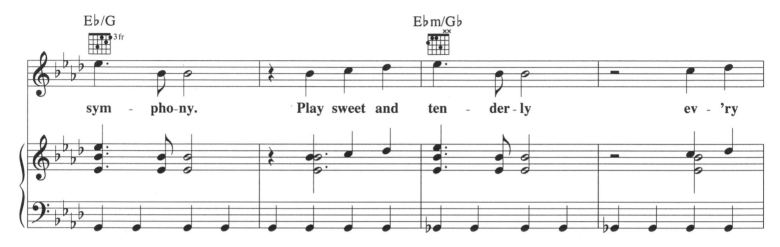

sym - pho-ny. Play sweet and ten - der-ly ev - 'ry

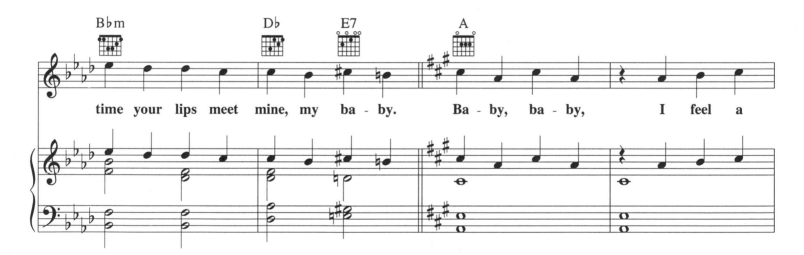

time your lips meet mine, my ba - by. Ba - by, ba - by, I feel a

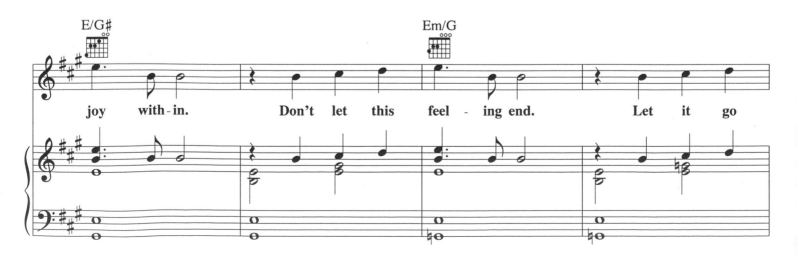

joy with-in. Don't let this feel - ing end. Let it go

may - be you'll go a - way __ and nev - er call, __ and a
may - be you think that love __ will make us fools, __ and

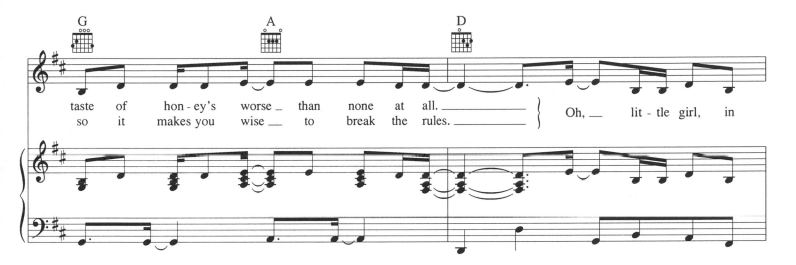

G   **A**   **D**

taste of hon - ey's worse __ than none at all. _____ Oh, __ lit - tle girl, in
so it makes you wise __ to break the rules. _____

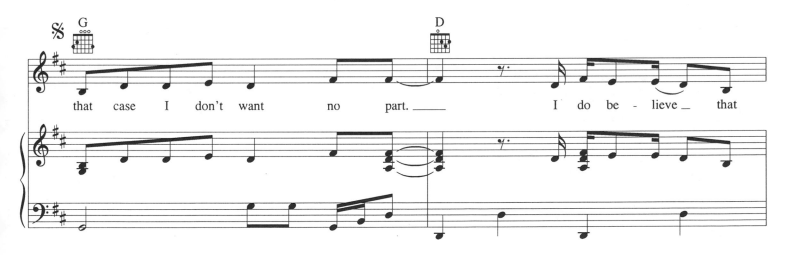

G   **D**

that case I don't want no part. _____ I do be - lieve __ that

G   **D**

that would on - ly break __ my heart. ___ Oh, _____ but

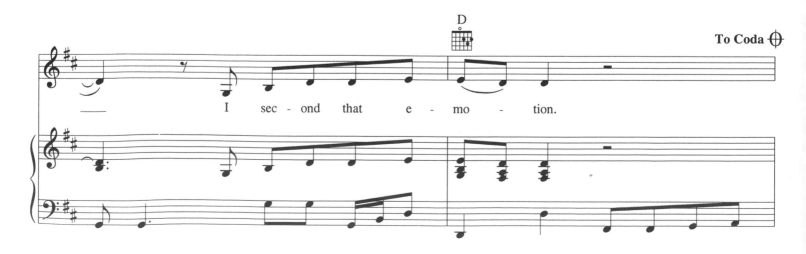

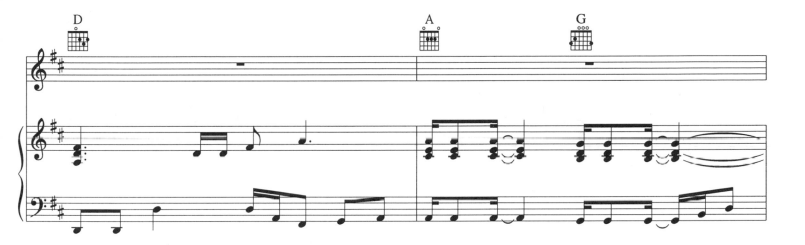

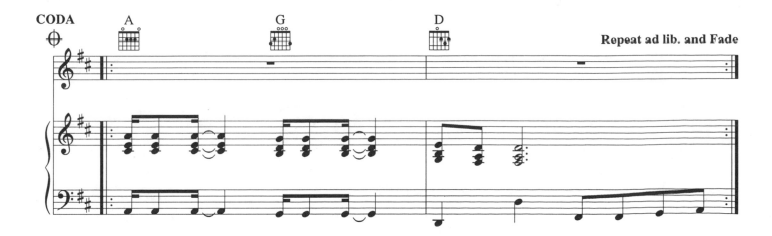

I'LL BE THERE

Words and Music by BERRY GORDY, HAL DAVIS,
WILLIE HUTCH and BOB WEST

51

Just call my name _____ and I'll _____ be there. _____

Just call my name _____

and I'll _____ be there. _____

IF I WERE YOUR WOMAN

Words and Music by LAVERNE WARE,
PAM SAWYER and CLAY McMURRAY

Moderate ballad, with a beat

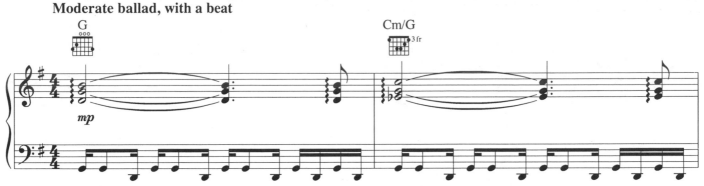

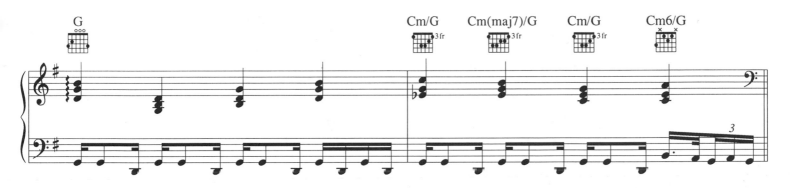

my love _ would o-ver-rule my sense and I'd call _ you back for more. If I were your

wom-an, if I were your wom-an, and you were my man.

She tears you down dar-lin' says you're noth-ing at all. __
Life _ is so cra-zy, and love _ is un-kind. _

But I'll pick you up dar-lin' when she let's you fall. You're _ like a dia-mond.
Be-cause she came first dar-lin', will she hang on your mind? You're _ a part of me.

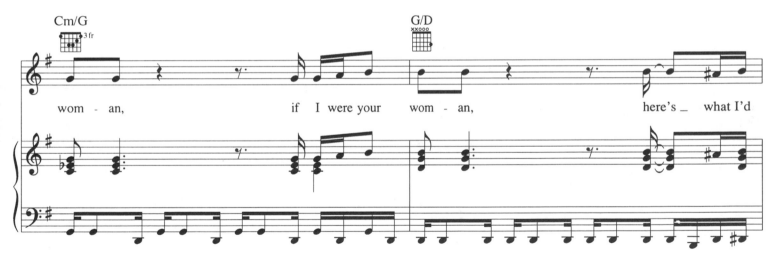

D.S. al Coda

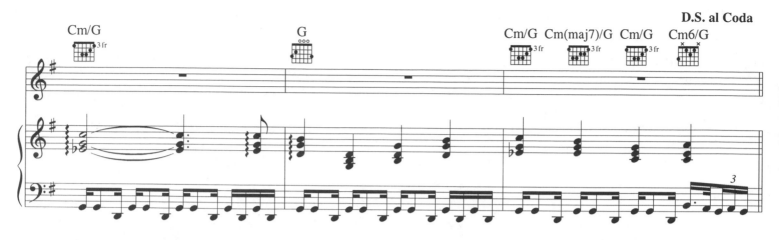

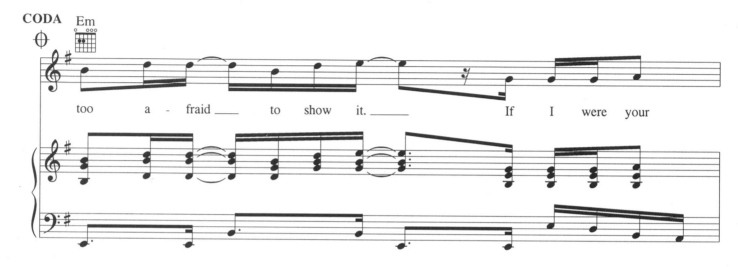

too a - fraid ___ to show it. ___ If I were your

wom - an, if I were your wom - an, if I were your

wom - an, here's ___ what I'd do; _____ I'd

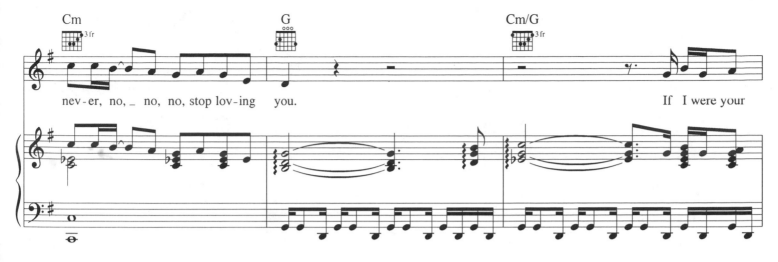

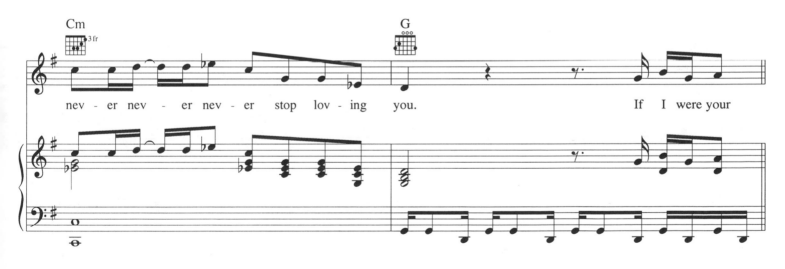

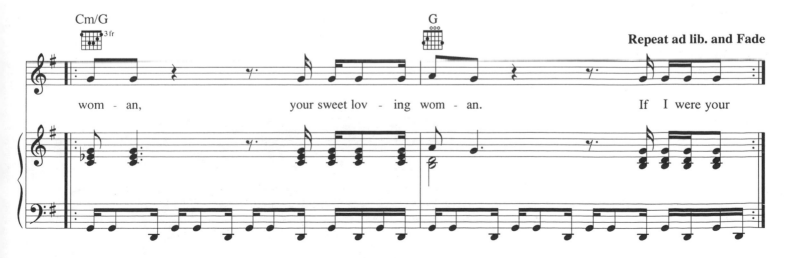

JUST MY IMAGINATION
(Running Away with Me)

Words and Music by NORMAN WHITFIELD
and BARRETT STRONG

To have a girl like her _____ is tru - ly
I tell you, I _____ can vis - ual -

a dream come _ true. _____
ize it _____ all. _____

Out of all the fel - lows in the
This could-n't be a dream, far too

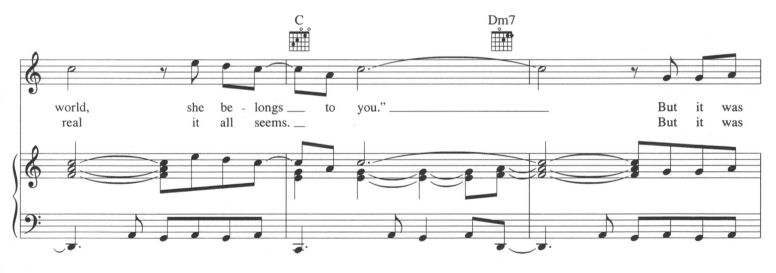

world, she be - longs ____ to you." _____ But it was
real it all seems. _ But it was

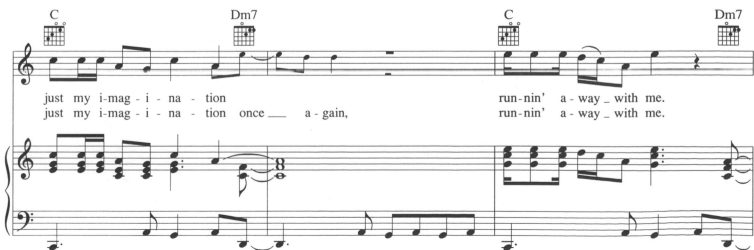

just my i-mag-i-na - tion run-nin' a - way _ with me.
just my i-mag-i-na - tion once ____ a - gain, run-nin' a - way _ with me.

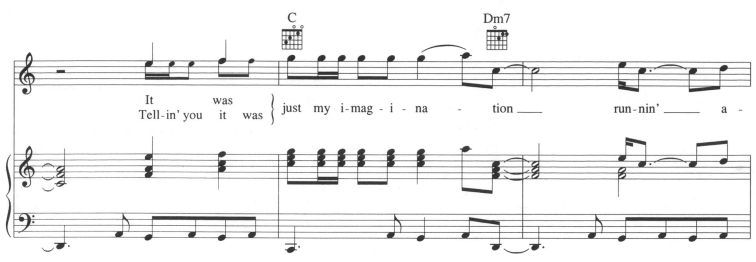

It was
Tell-in' you it was { just my i-mag-i-na - tion run-nin' a-

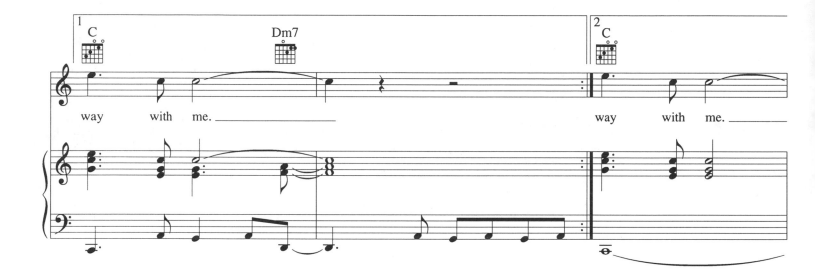

way with me. _____   way with me. _____

_____ Ev - 'ry night _ on my

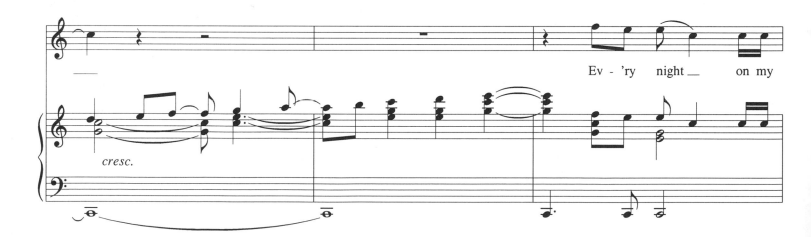

cresc.

knees I pray, _____   ("Dear Lord,) _ hear my plea. _____

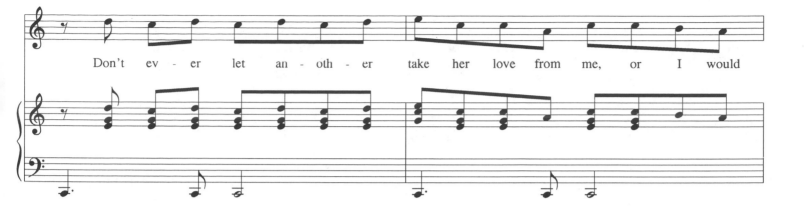

Don't ev-er let an-oth-er take her love from me, or I would

G7   C

sure-ly die." _____ Her love is heav-en-ly.

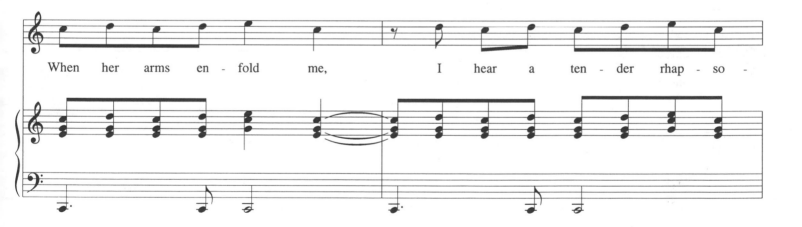

When her arms en-fold me, I hear a ten-der rhap-so-

dy. But in re-al-i-ty, she does-n't e-ven know me. _

just my i-mag-i-na-tion, once ____ a - gain,

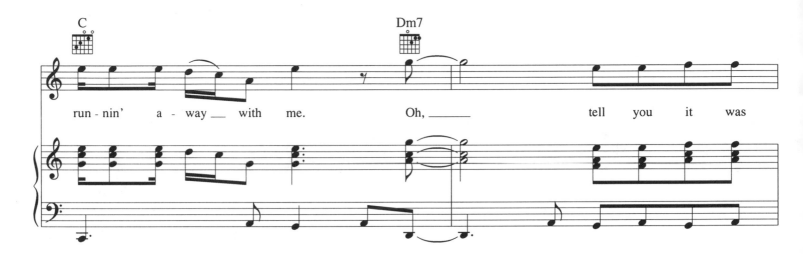

run-nin' a-way ____ with me. Oh, _____ tell you it was

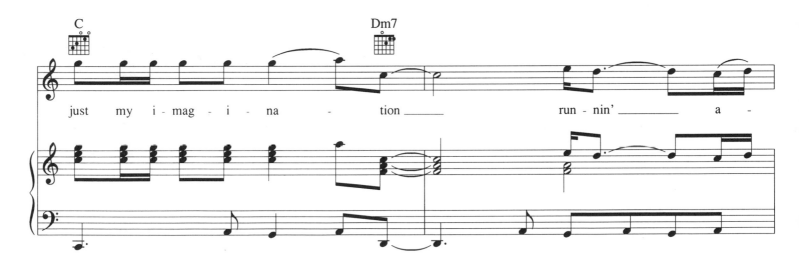

just my i-mag-i-na ____ tion _____ run-nin' _____ a -

Repeat and Fade

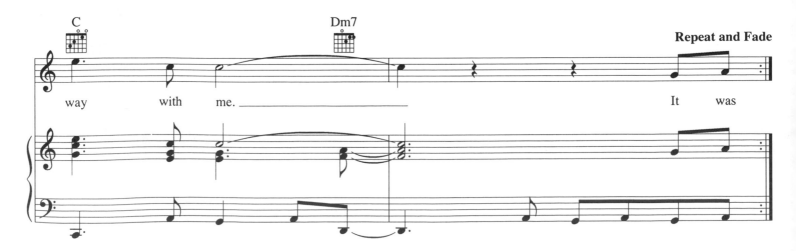

way with me. _____ It was

LET'S GET IT ON

Words and Music by MARVIN GAYE
and ED TOWNSEND

Slow Soul beat

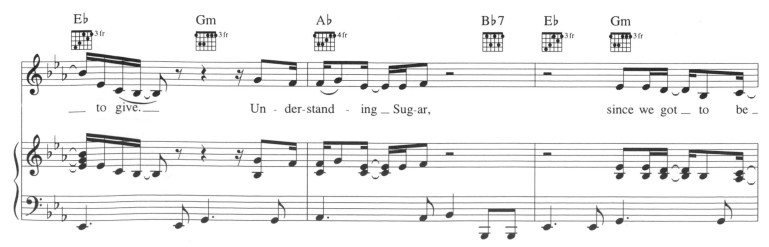

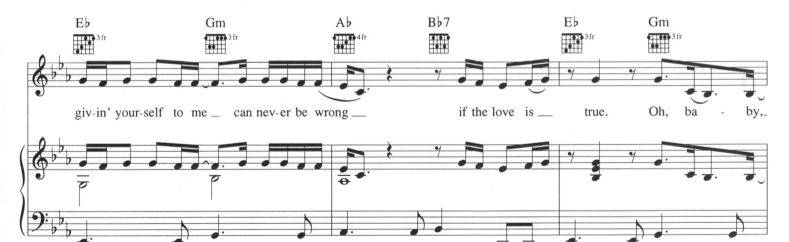

_ ooh. _ I'm _ ask - in' you, _ ba - by, to get it on with me._

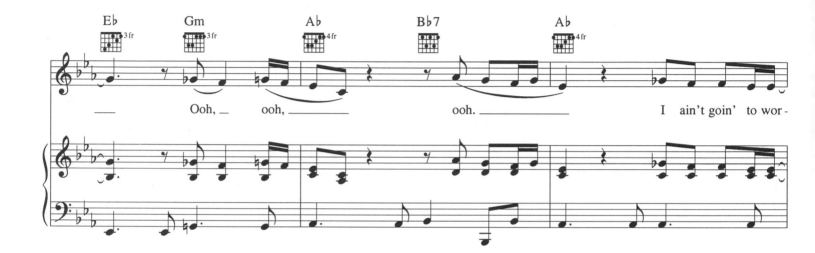

_ Ooh, _ ooh, _ ooh. _ I ain't goin' to wor-

-ry. _ I ain't goin' to push. _ I won't push you, ba - by. Just

come on, come on, come on, _ come on, come on ba - by, _ stop beat-in' 'round _ the _ bush. Hey,_

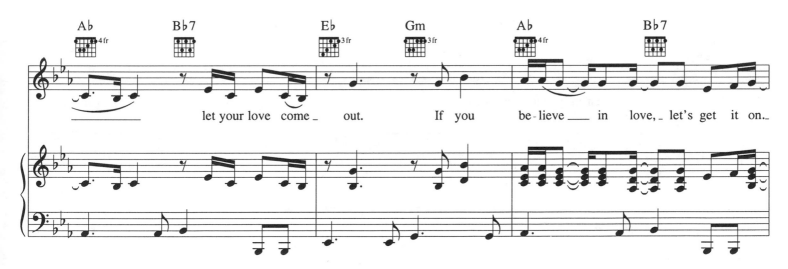

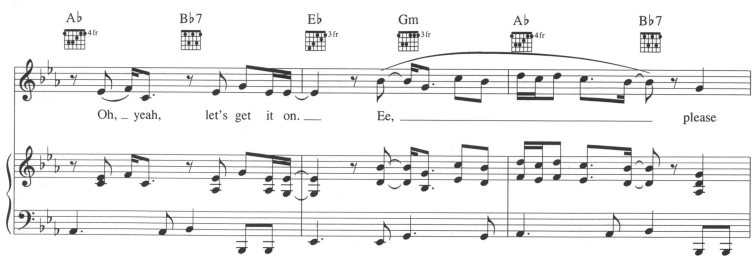

Oh, _ yeah, let's get it on. _ Ee, _____ please

get it on. _ Hey, _____ hey. _____ Come on, come on, come on, _ come on, come on, dar -

- lin', _ stop beat-in' 'round _ the bush. _____ Oh, gon-na get it on. _

_____ Right with you, _ ba - by, I _ want to get it on. _ You don't have _ to wor-

-ry that it's wrong.___ If the spi-rit moves_you, let me groove_you. Good,_ let your love come_

down, oh. Get it on,___ come on,___ ba-by. Do you know I

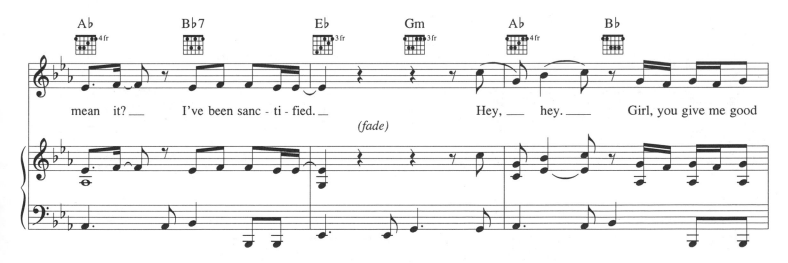

mean it?___ I've been sanc-ti-fied.___ *(fade)* Hey,___ hey.___ Girl, you give me good

feel-ings,___ so good,___ some-thin' like sum-mer-time.___

MAYBE TOMORROW

Words and Music by BERRY GORDY JR., ALPHONSO J. MIZELL, FREDERICK J. PERREN and DEKE RICHARDS

I don't know how man-y stars____ there are up in the heav-en-ly sky.____

I on-ly know my heav-en is here____ on earth each

MERCY, MERCY ME
(The Ecology)

Words and Music by
MARVIN GAYE

1. Woo ___ ah ___ mer-cy, mer-cy me. ___ Ah, ___ things
2. *(See additional lyrics)*

___ ain't what ___ they used ___ to be. ___ No, ___ no, ___ where did all ___ the blue ___ skies ___ go, ___

poi-son is the wind ___ that blows ___ from the north ___ and south ___ and east. Woo ___ mer-

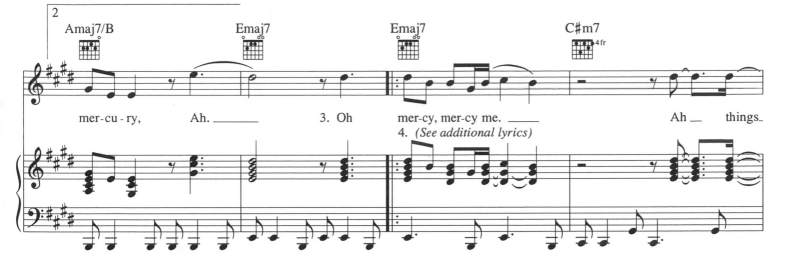

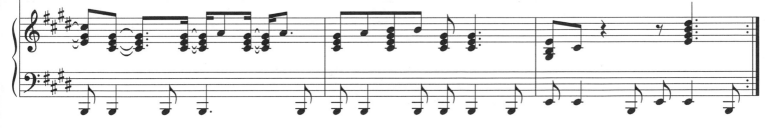

my sweet _ Lord, no, no, na, na, na,

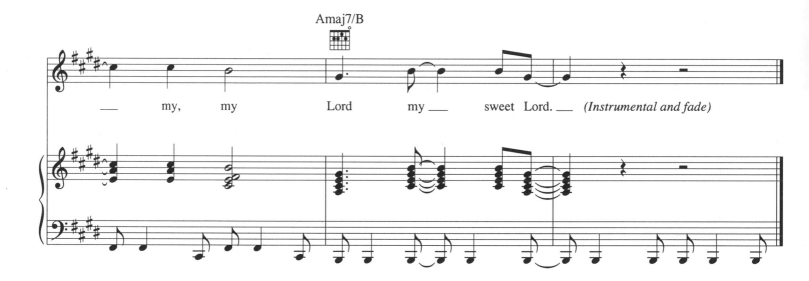

— my, my Lord my ___ sweet Lord. ___ *(Instrumental and fade)*

Additional Lyrics

2. Ah things ain't what they used to be, no, no
   Oil wasted on the ocean and upon
   Our seas fish full of mercury, Ah.

4. Ah things ain't what they used to be
   What about this overcrowded land
   How much more abuse from man can she stand?

MY GIRL

Words and Music by WILLIAM "SMOKEY" ROBINSON
and RONALD WHITE

I've got sun - shine

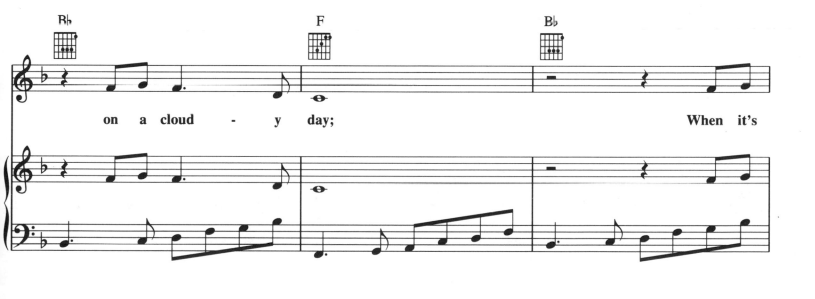

on a cloud - y day;   When it's

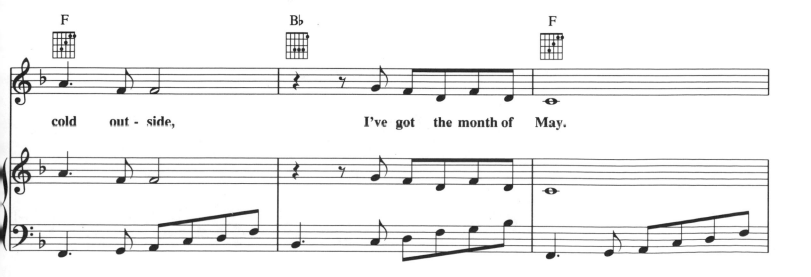

cold out - side,   I've got the month of May.

I guess you say, What can make me

feel this way? My girl, _____ talk-ing 'bout my _ girl. _____

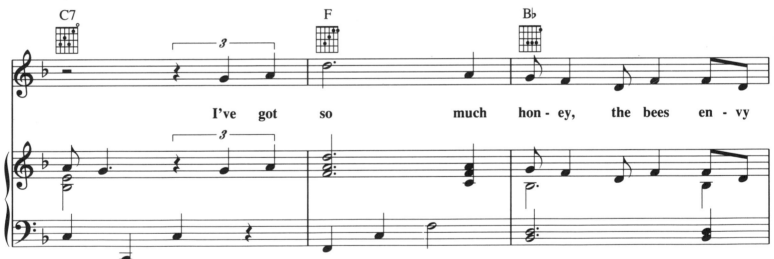

I've got so much hon-ey, the bees en-vy

me; I've got a sweet-er song _____

NEVER CAN SAY GOODBYE

Words and Music by
CLIFTON DAVIS

SOMEDAY WE'LL BE TOGETHER

Words and Music by JACKEY BEAVERS,
JOHNNY BRISTOL and HARVEY FUQUA

86

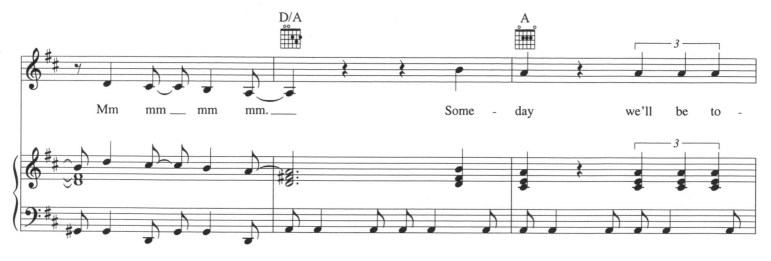

REACH OUT AND TOUCH
(Somebody's Hand)

Words and Music by NICKOLAS ASHFORD
and VALERIE SIMPSON

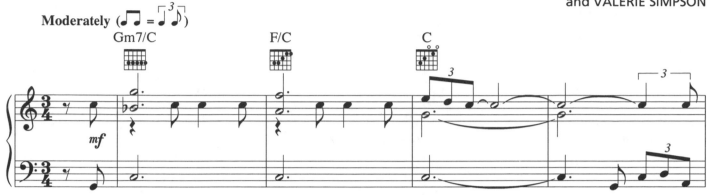

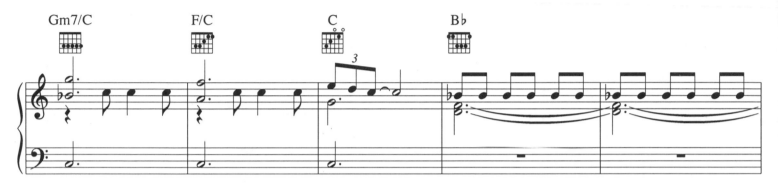

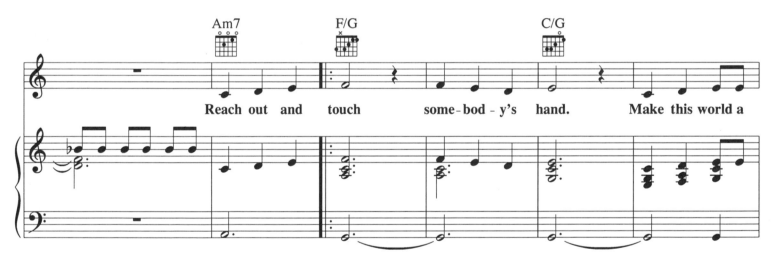

Reach out and touch some-bod-y's hand. Make this world a

bet-ter place if you can. Reach out and touch

93

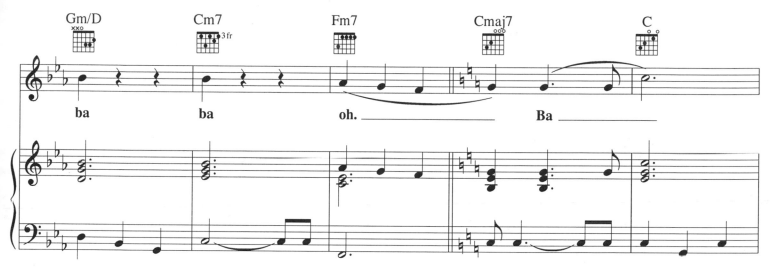

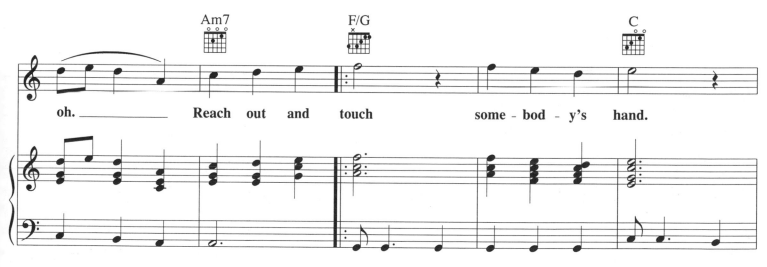

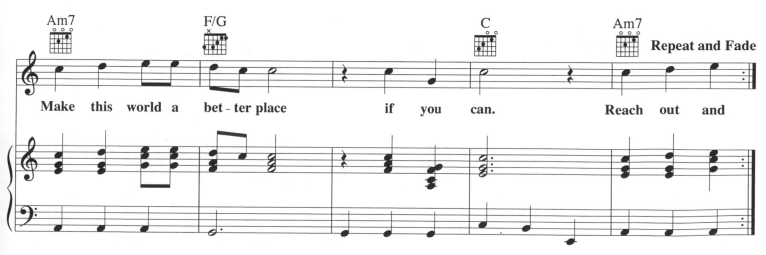

SMILING FACES SOMETIMES

Words and Music by NORMAN WHITFIELD
and BARRETT STRONG

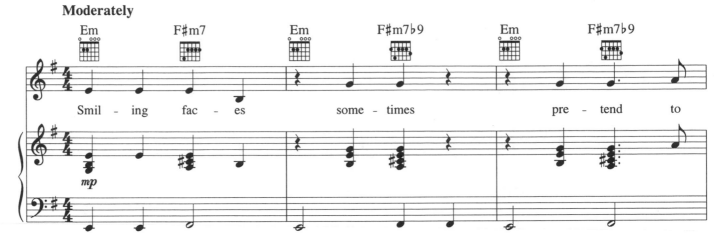

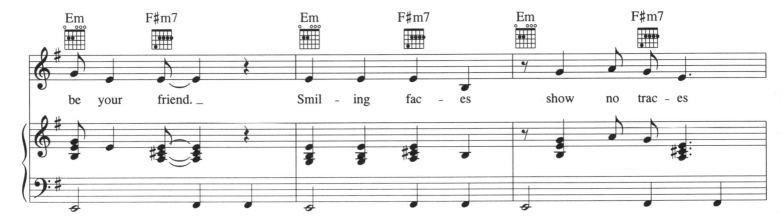

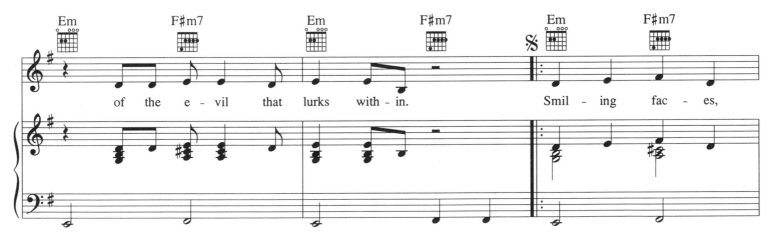

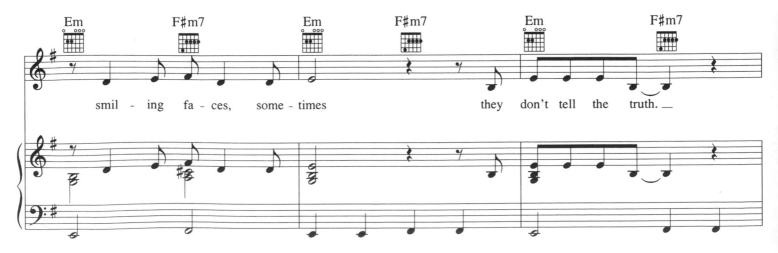

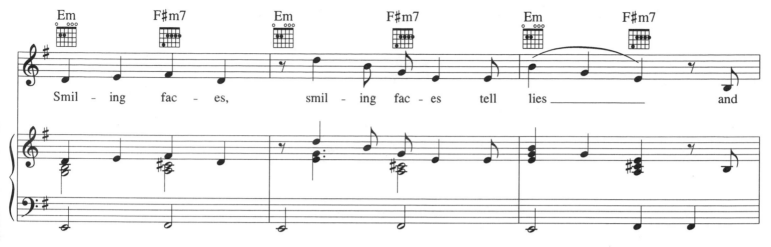

Smil - ing fac - es, smil - ing fac - es tell lies _____ and

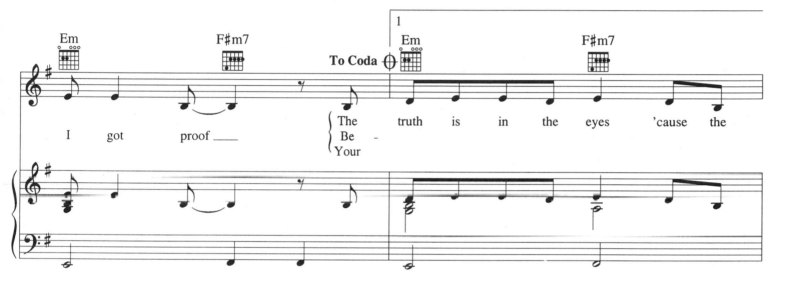

I got proof ____

To Coda ⊕

The truth is in the eyes 'cause the
Be -
Your

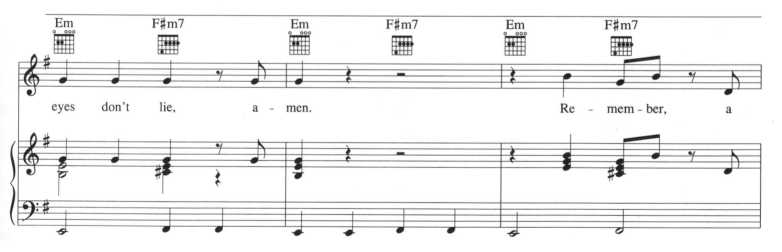

eyes don't lie, a - men. Re - mem - ber, a

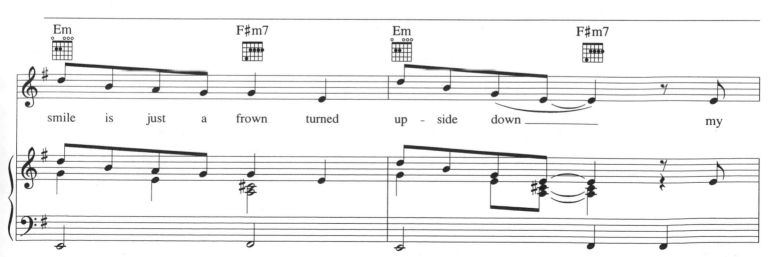

smile is just a frown turned up - side down _____ my

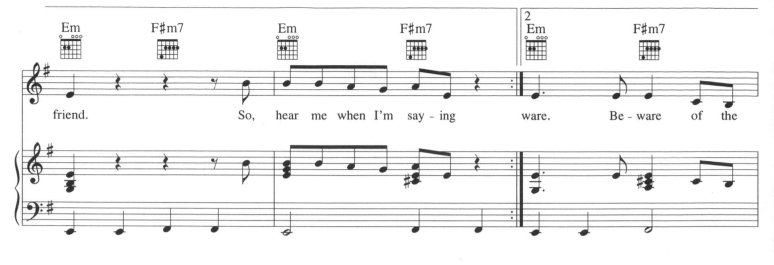

friend.   So,   hear me when I'm say - ing   ware.   Be - ware of the

hand - shake   that hides the snake.   I'm   tell - in' you

be - ware of the pat on the back   it   just   might

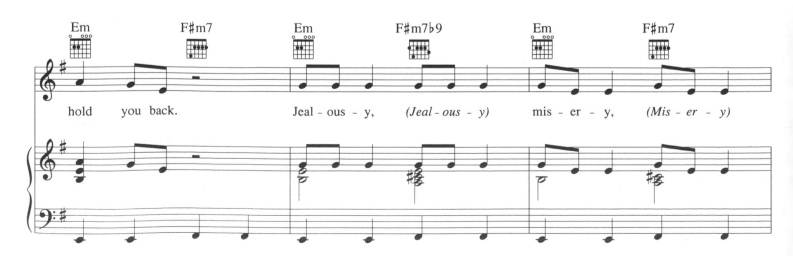

hold   you back.   Jeal - ous - y,   (Jeal - ous - y)   mis - er - y,   (Mis - er - y)

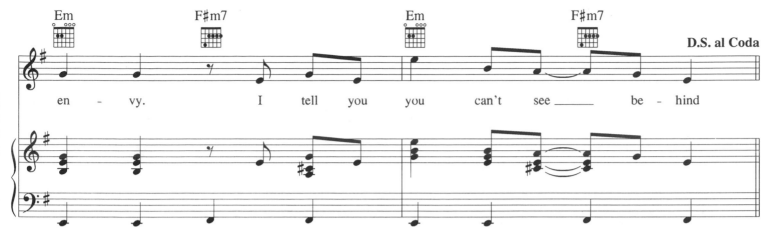

en - vy. I tell you you can't see _____ be - hind

en - e - my won't do you no harm, _ 'cause you'll know where he's

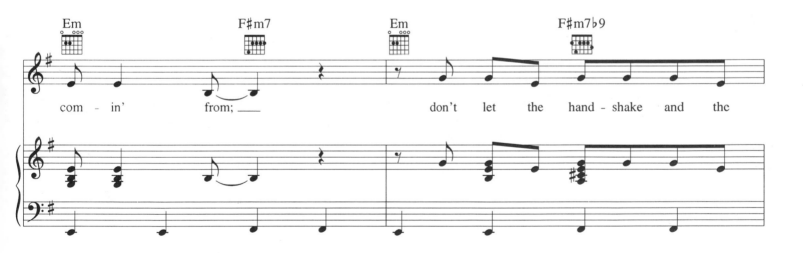

com - in' from; _____ don't let the hand - shake and the

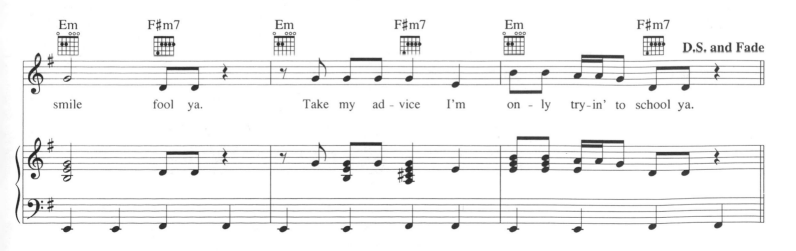

smile fool ya. Take my ad - vice I'm on - ly try-in' to school ya.

STILL

Words and Music by
LIONEL RICHIE

but then, most of all, _____ I do love ___ you ___

To Coda

Whispered: *still.*

rit.

f
a tempo

D.S. al Coda

We played the

CODA

THREE TIMES A LADY

Words and Music by
LIONEL RICHIE

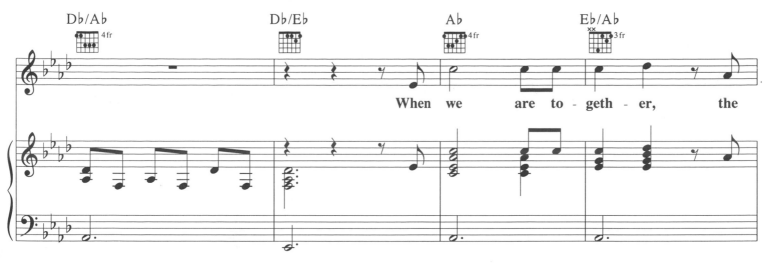

When we are to - geth - er, the

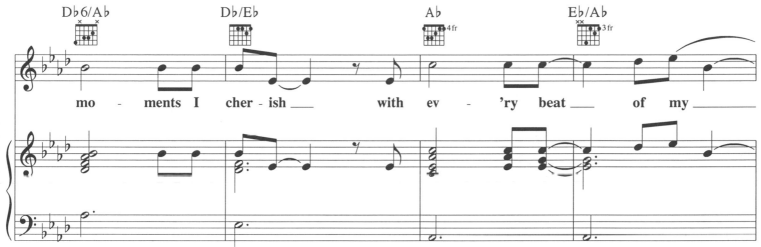

mo - ments I cher - ish ___ with ev - 'ry beat ___ of my ___

___ heart; _____ To touch you, to hold you, to

feel you, to need you, ___ there's noth - ing to keep us a -

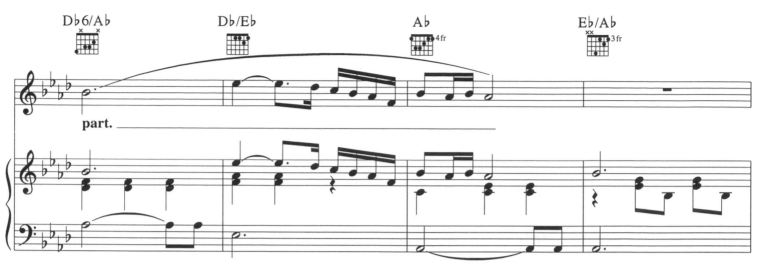

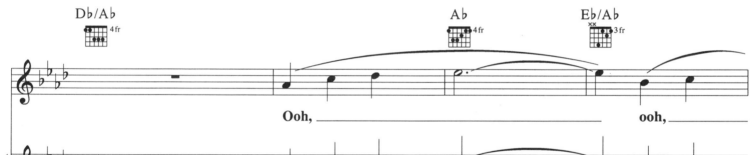

TIME WILL REVEAL

Words and Music by BUNNY DeBARGE
and ELDRA DeBARGE

But this time love's _ for real. _ In time it will _ re - veal. _

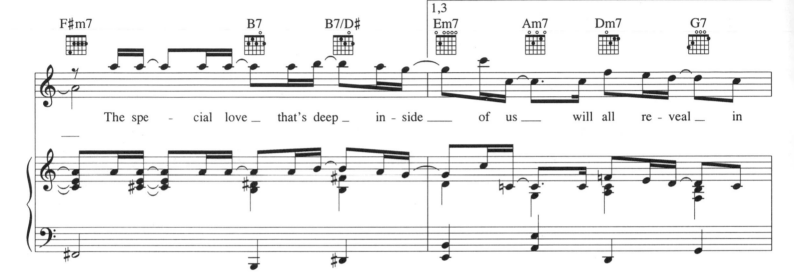

The spe - cial love _ that's deep _ in - side _ of us _ will all re - veal _ in

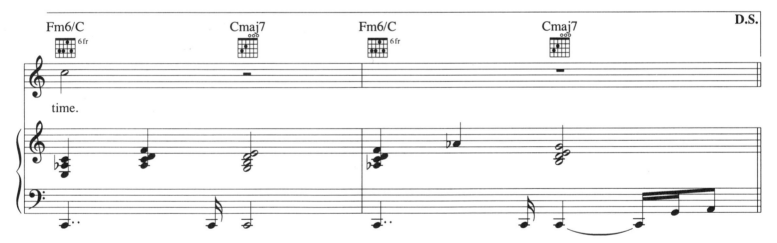

time.

D.S.

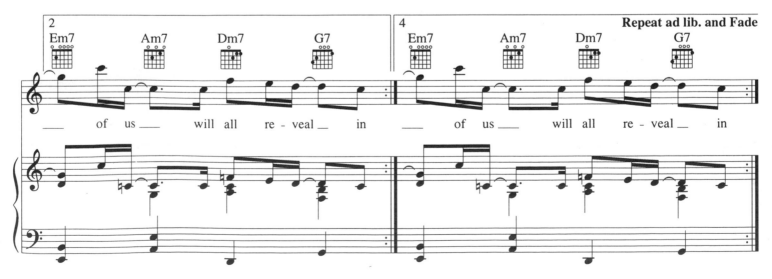

_ of us _ will all re - veal _ in _ of us _ will all re - veal _ in

Repeat ad lib. and Fade

TOUCH ME IN THE MORNING

Words and Music by RONALD MILLER
and MICHAEL MASSER

THE TRACKS OF MY TEARS

Words and Music by WILLIAM "SMOKEY" ROBINSON,
WARREN MOORE and MARVIN TARPLIN

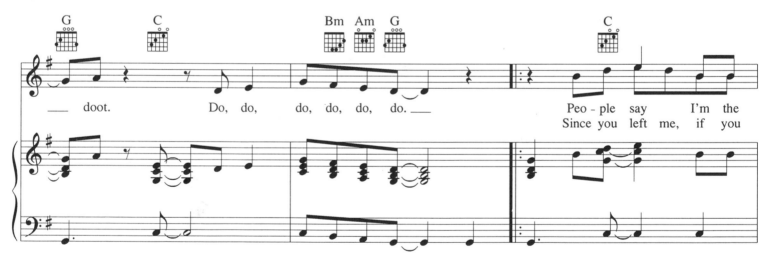

Do, do, do, ___ doot.   Do, do, do, ___ doot.   Do, do, do,

___ doot.   Do, do, do, do, do, do. ___   Peo - ple say   I'm the
                                               Since you left me, if you

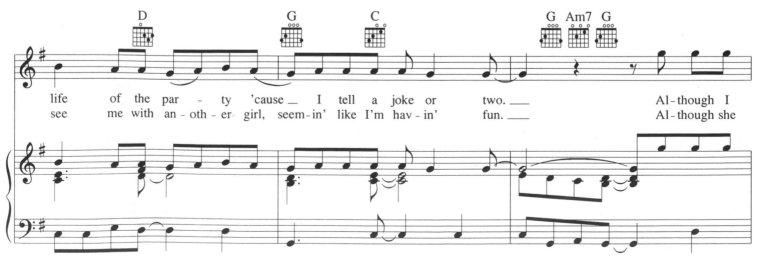

life   of the par - ty 'cause ___ I tell a joke or   two. ___   Al - though I
see   me with an - oth - er girl, seem - in' like I'm hav - in'   fun. ___   Al - though she

might be _____ laugh - in' loud _____ and heart - y,
may be _____ cute, she's just a sub - sti - tute be - cause

deep in - side ___ I'm blue. ___
you're the per - ma - nent one. ___ } So take a good look at my

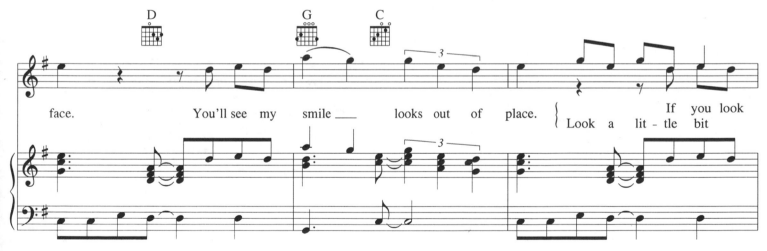

face. You'll see my smile ___ looks out of place.
{ Look a lit - tle bit If you look

clos - er } it's eas - y to trace the tracks of __ my _____ tears. ___
clos - er,

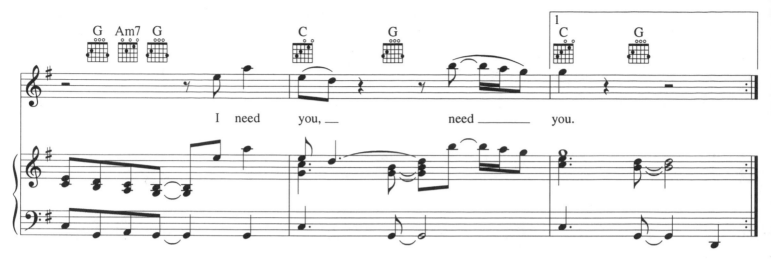

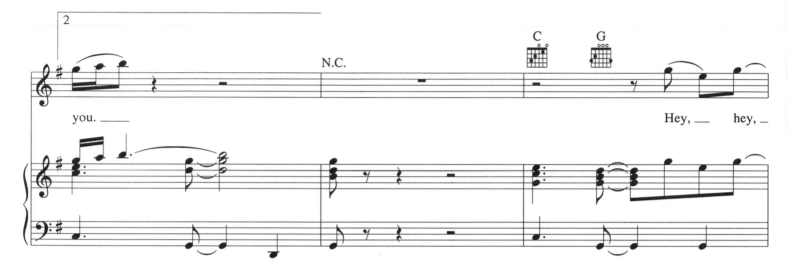

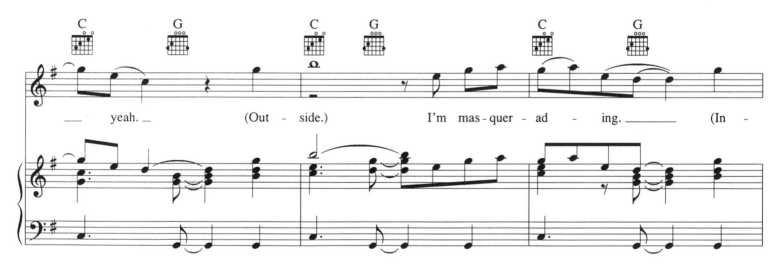

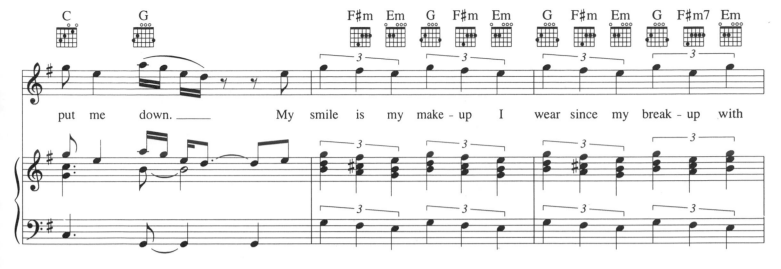

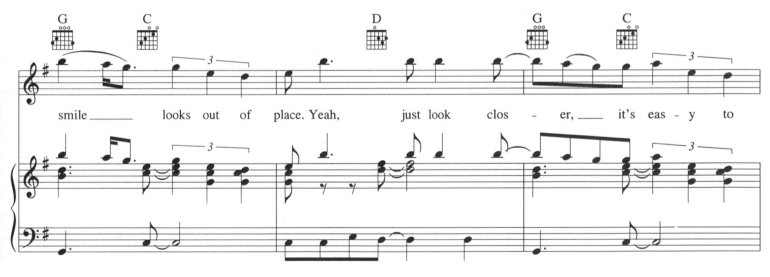

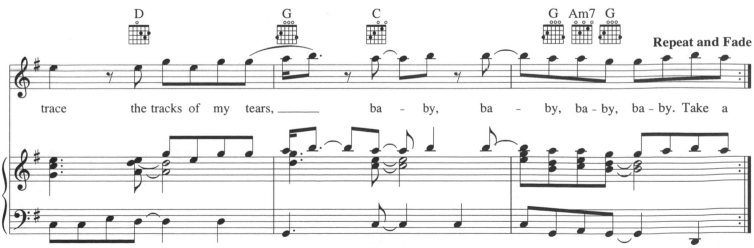

WHAT'S GOING ON

Words and Music by MARVIN GAYE,
AL CLEVELAND and RENALDO BENSON

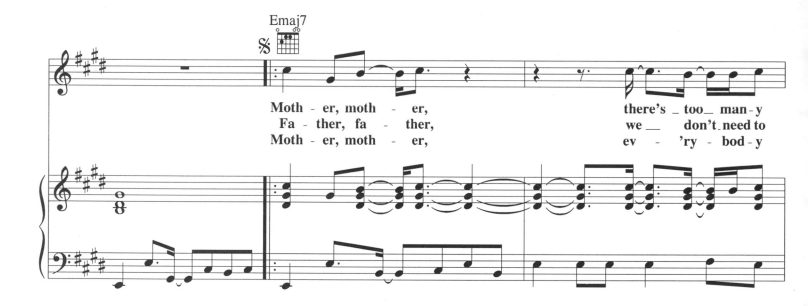

Moth - er, moth - er, there's _ too _ man - y
Fa - ther, fa - ther, we _ don't need to
Moth - er, moth - er, ev - 'ry - bod - y

of you cry - ing. Broth-er, broth - er, broth - er,
es - ca - late. _____ You see, _ war is not _ the an - swer,
thinks we're wrong. _ Ah, but _ who are they _ to judge _ us

ah, ah.

I, ___ yi, yi, yi, ___ yi, yi, ___ yi, ya, ___ ya, ya, ___ ya.

I, ___ yi, yi, ___ yi, yi, ___ yi, ya, ___ ya, ya, ___ ya, ya. ___

ya, ya, ya.

I, yi, yi, yi, yi, yi, ya, ya, ya, ya, ya.

A/B

Be, doot, de, doot; Be, be, be, doot; Be be, be, doot;

Repeat and Fade

Bu, doot, be, be, be, doot; Be be, be, be, be, doot. Ooh,

WHERE DID OUR LOVE GO

Words and Music by BRIAN HOLLAND,
LAMONT DOZIER and EDDIE HOLLAND

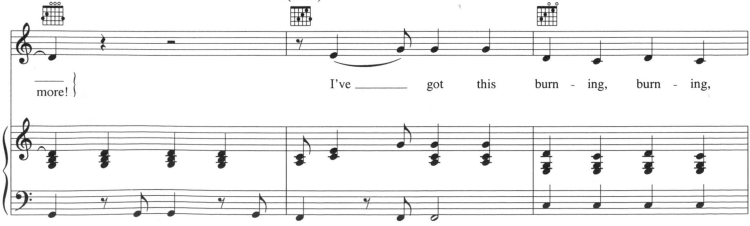

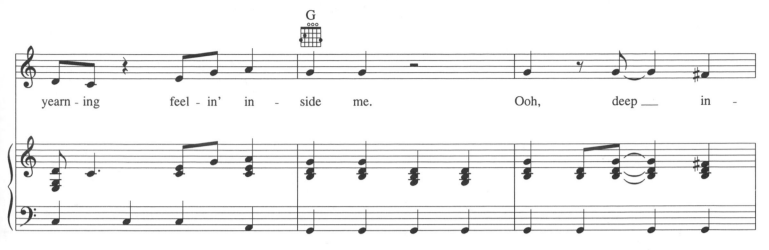

yearn - ing   feel - in' in - side me.   Ooh,   deep ___ in -

side   me   and it hurts ___ so ___ bad.

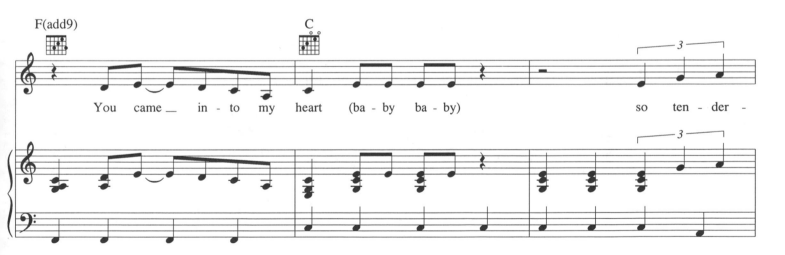

You came ___ in - to my heart (ba - by ba - by)   so ten - der -

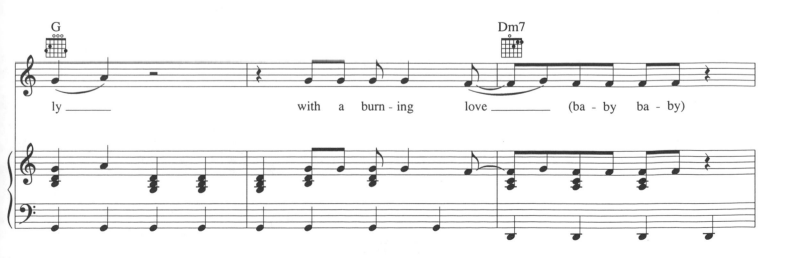

ly ___   with a burn - ing   love ___ (ba - by ba - by)

G7   F(add9)

Don't you want me no more? (ba-by ba-by)   Ooh,   ba - by.

C   G

Dm7   G

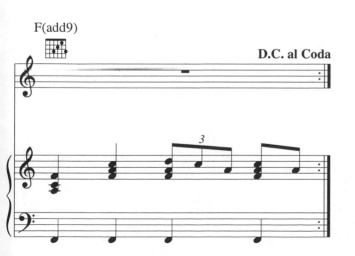

F(add9)   D.C. al Coda

CODA   F(add9)

Be - fore ___ you won my

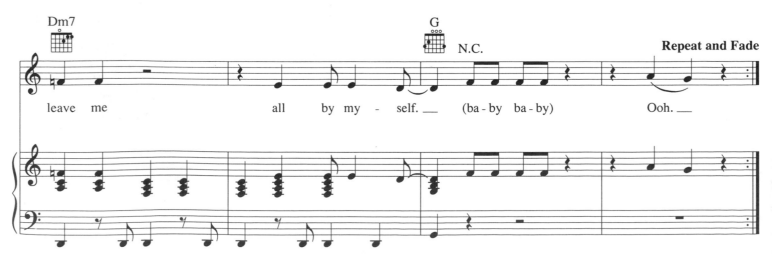

YOU'RE ALL I NEED TO GET BY

Words and Music by NICKOLAS ASHFORD
and VALERIE SIMPSON

Moderately

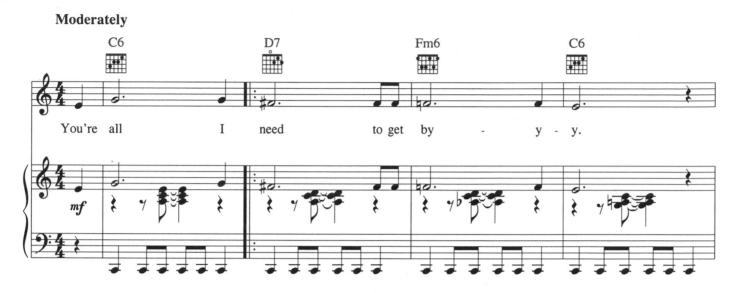

You're all   I need   to get   by - y - y.

(Boy) Like the sweet   morn-ing dew,   I took one look at you,   and it was plain _ to see
(Boy) Like an ea-gle pro-tects his nest   for you I'll do my best,   stand by you like _ a tree,

you were my des - ti - ny. (Girl) With my arms   o-pen wide, _   I threw a-way _ my pride.
dare an-y-bod-y to try and move me. (Girl) Dar-lin' in   you I found _   strength where I was _ torn down.

that's e- nough.__ You're all,   you're all I need __   to get by. __
-mi - na - tion. __ You're

I   all,   you're all   I   want to strive for and do__ a lit -tle more.

All,   all the joys   un-der the sun wrapp'd up __ in - to one. You're   all,   you're all I

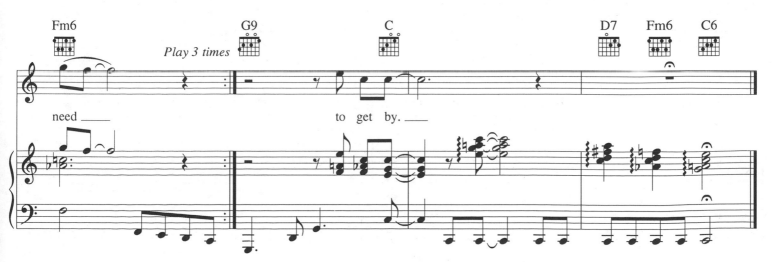

need ___   to get by. ___

Play 3 times

YOU'VE REALLY GOT A HOLD ON ME

Slowly

Words and Music by
WILLIAM "SMOKEY" ROBINSON

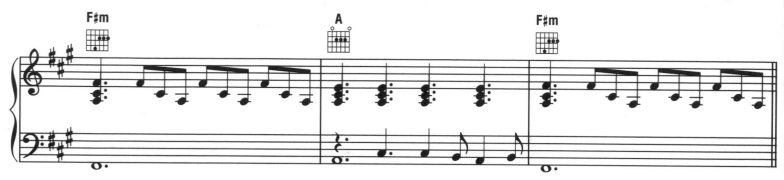

I don't____ like you,____ but I____ love you;
I don't____ want you,____ but I____ need you;
I wan - na leave you,____ don't wan - na stay here;

Seems that I'm al - ways____ think - ing of you.____
Don't wan - na kiss you,____ but I____ need to.____
Don't wan - na spend____ an - oth - er day here.____

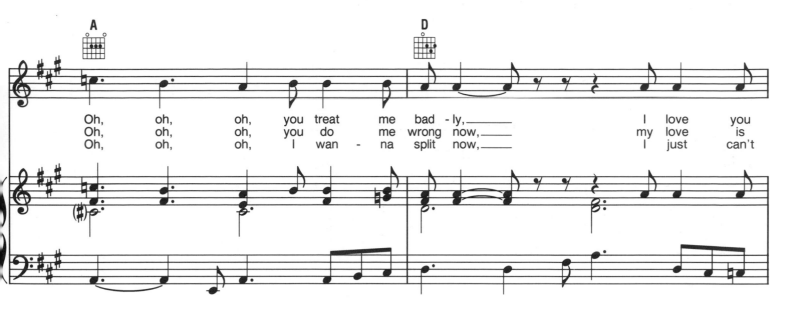

A   **D**

Oh,   oh,   oh,   you treat me bad - ly,_____   I love you
Oh,   oh,   oh,   you do me wrong now,_____   my love is
Oh,   oh,   oh,   I wan - na split now,_____   I just can't

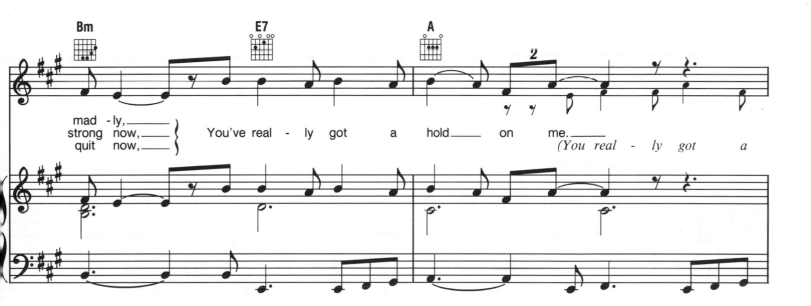

Bm   **E7**   **A**   **2**

mad - ly,_____
strong now,_____   You've real - ly got a hold____ on me._____
quit now,_____   *(You real - ly got a*

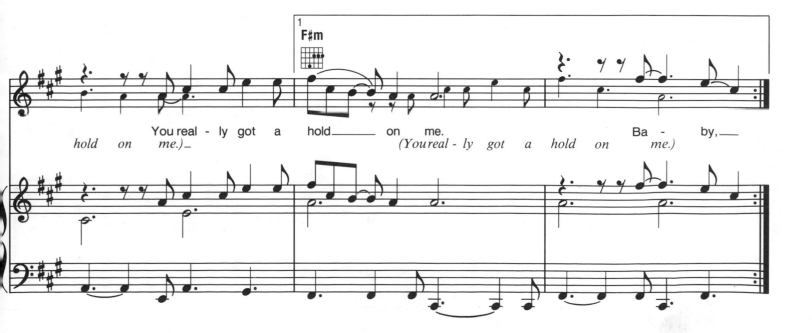

1   **F#m**

      You real - ly got a hold_____ on me.   Ba - by,____
*hold on me.)_*   *(You real - ly got a hold on me.)*

You've Made Me So Very Happy

Words and Music by BERRY GORDY, FRANK WILSON,
BRENDA HOLLOWAY and PATRICE HOLLOWAY